eat your
greens
reds
yellows
and
purples

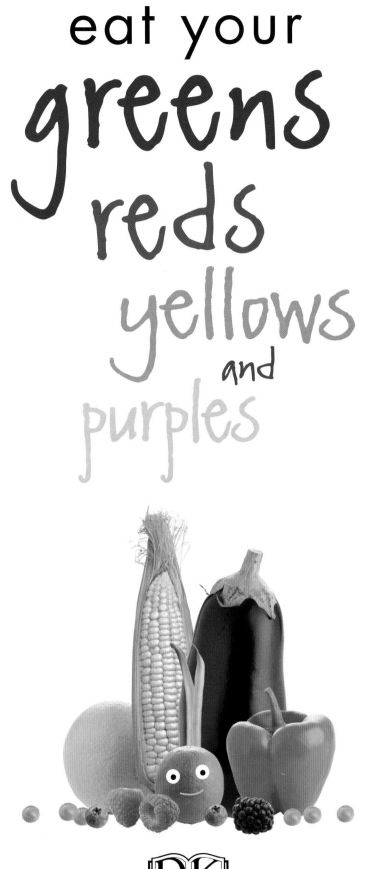

Penguin Random House

Editors James Mitchem, Carrie Love
Senior designer Sadie Thomas
Editorial assistant Sophia Danielsson-Waters
Art direction for photography Charlotte Bull
Photographer Dave King
Food stylist Georgie Besterman
Nutritional consultant Fiona Hunter
Recipe consultant Lorna Rhodes
Senior producer Leila Green
Producer, Pre-Production Dragana Puvacic
Jacket designer Amy Keast
Jacket coordinator Francesca Young
Creative technical support Sonia Charbonnier
Managing editor Penny Smith
Managing art editor Gemma Glover
Art director Jane Bull
Publisher Mary Ling

First published in Great Britain in 2016 by
Dorling Kindersley Limited
80 Strand, London WC2R 0RL

Copyright © 2016 Dorling Kindersley Limited
A Penguin Random House Company
10 9 8 7 6 5 4 3 2 1
001–291661–Apr/16

A CIP catalogue record for this book
is available from the British Library.
ISBN: 978–0–2412–5022–8
Printed in China.
All images © Dorling Kindersley Limited
For further information see: www.dkimages.com

A WORLD OF IDEAS
SEE ALL THERE IS TO KNOW

www.dk.com

THE MENU

GET COOKING

Here's a guide to the equipment used in this book. Obviously you'll only need certain items for each recipe, so read through each one before you begin to make sure you have what you need.

SAFETY RULES

1. **ALWAYS ASK AN ADULT** for help with anything hot or sharp.

2. **WASH YOUR HANDS** to help prevent the spread of germs.

3. **KEEP A TIDY KITCHEN** and wipe up spills that could cause accidents.

KEY TO THE SYMBOLS USED IN THE RECIPES

PREP TIME
How long a recipe will take to prepare (includes chilling etc.)

COOKING TIME
How much time each recipe will take to actually cook.

SERVES
How many people the recipe will serve, or how many portions it makes.

SAFETY
Take extra special care and ask an adult for help.

Large ovenproof dish

Pots (variety of sizes)

Lasagne dish

Mixing bowls

Baking trays

Baking sheet

Muffin tray

Roasting tray

Cutlery

Pastry brush

Sharp knife

Cocktail stick

Chopsticks

Garlic Crusher

4

Baking paper

Cling film

Tin foil

Oven gloves

Tea towels

Airtight containers

Bowls

Glasses

Mugs

Plates

Saucepans (with lids)

Colander

Non-stick frying pan

Griddle pan

Scales

Measuring spoons

Measuring cups

Jugs

Grater

Wok

Sieve

23cm (9in) square cake tin

Chopping board

Lolly moulds

Blender

Food processor

Loaf tin

Plastic bags

Muffin cases

Electric whisk

Flipper

Serving spoon

Rolling pin

Peeler

Ladle

Wooden spoon

Spatula

Potato masher

Hand whisk

5

EAT YOUR GREENS

GREEN food is packed with VITAMINS, FIBRE, and other goodies that help keep your body healthy and strong. Some of these things are hard to find in other food, so the more peas, broccoli, spinach, and beans you eat, the better!

AND YOUR REDS

RED food can be a good source of vitamins that help protect your body's cells. So be sure to eat your fill of tomatoes, radishes, cherries, berries, and watermelon.

Vitamin A

Vitamin C

AND YOUR PURPLES

PURPLE food such as blackberries, blueberries, red cabbage, raisins, aubergines, plums, and grapes can contain chemicals that help protect your body from DISEASE and keep your heart healthy.

AND YOUR YELLOWS

YELLOW food usually contains lots of Vitamin A and C. So by eating plenty of corn, lemons, bananas, peppers, melon, apricots, and pineapple, you will boost your body's IMMUNE SYSTEM, which is what makes sure you stay well.

AND YOUR ORANGES

ORANGE food such as carrots, sweet potatoes, squash, pumpkin, and – of course – oranges can contain something called CAROTENES. These are converted to Vitamin A, which help keeps your eyes, skin, hair, bones, and teeth in good shape.

Vitamin B

Vitamin C

EAT A
RAINBOW

Meet the stars of the show! Fruit and veg are packed with wonderful things your body needs. Every colour is good in different ways – whether it's helping you grow big and strong, stopping you from getting ill, or giving you energy. So don't just stop at one or two! Fill your plate with a rainbow of flavour.

Garlic

Pineapple

Onion

Potato

Lime

Avocado

Rocket

Kale

Leeks

Yellow pepper

Lemon

Celery

Peas

Green pepper

Broccoli

Bananas

Sweetcorn

Courgette

Asparagus

Ginger

Spring onions

Green beans

Green grapes

Spinach

Cucumber

Honeydew melon

Sweet potato

Grapefruits

How many have you
TRIED?

Butternut
squash

Tangerine

Chillies

Red pepper

Papayas

Strawberries

Apple

Blackberries

Blueberries

Peaches

Orange pepper

Raspberries

Cherries

Aubergine

Beetroot

Oranges

Carrot

Watermelon

Raisins

Red cabbage

Apricot

Pumpkin

Tomatoes

Red onion

Figs

Red grapes

Plum

PREPARING YOUR INGREDIENTS

Your fruit and veg need a little love and care before they're ready to be used. There are lots of ways to prepare them, but these basic skills are bound to be useful again and again.

GINGER

TAKE A PIECE OF GINGER and use a teaspoon to scrape off the skin. Then either rub the ginger on a grater or cut it into slices.

POTATOES

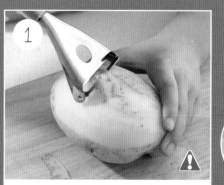

USE A PEELER to remove the skin, then rinse the potatoes in cold water. You can prepare sweet potatoes the same way.

CAREFULLY CUT THE POTATO into whichever shape you need. This could be little chunks, wedges, slices, or batons (for chips).

BROCCOLI

HOLD THE BROCCOLI by the stalk. Carefully go around the stalk with a knife, trimming off the florets (little trees). Then slice the stalk.

GARLIC

FIRMLY PUSH DOWN on a bulb of garlic to break it into segments (cloves). Press down on the cloves with a knife to loosen the papery peel.

PLACE THE CLOVES in a garlic crusher and squeeze. If you need slices, ask an adult for help, as garlic has to be sliced very thinly.

CARROTS

USE A PEELER TO remove the skin, then either grate or cut the carrots into rounds or batons (little rectangles that look like chips).

AVOCADOS

1 CAREFULLY CUT AROUND the outside of the avocado, then twist the two halves to separate them.

2 USE A SPOON to remove the stone, then either peel off the skin or scoop out the flesh.

TOMATOES

1 CAREFULLY CUT YOUR TOMATOES in half, then use a spoon to scoop out all the seeds.

PEPPERS

1 CUT THE PEPPER in half from top to bottom. Remove the stalk, seeds and white pith.

2 CAREFULLY SLICE THE PEPPER into strips, chunks, or cubes, depending on the recipe.

COURGETTES

1 TRIM BOTH ENDS of the courgette and either cut into rounds, or cut in half lengthways then slice into half moon shapes.

ONIONS

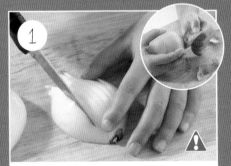

1 PEEL THE ONION and slice it in half from root to stem. Make several slices toward the root, but don't cut all the way to the end.

2 MAKE SIDEWAYS CUTS towards the root – once near the bottom and once near the top.

3 HOLDING THE ONION together, cut down across the cuts. This will separate the onion into little cubes. This is known as "dicing".

MEET THE GREENS

HOWDY ALL! First up there's bold broccoli, then there's amazing avocado, followed by luscious lime, powerful peas, great green beans, and last but not least, strong spinach! Greens are good for your overall health and in particular your blood and heart.

Broccoli contains almost as much Vitamin C as oranges.

We're the GREEN TEAM

I'm high in antioxidants, which help to slow down wear and tear on your body's cells.

GREENS ARE GOOD

There's a reason that people are always saying "eat your greens". Green food is often full of Vitamin K and other goodies that your body needs to stay healthy. (Sadly, this doesn't include green sweets!)

B vitamins

Cooked spinach contains LESS nutrition than when it is raw, but it's still great!

Spring onions are also called "scallions" or "salad onions". They are full of goodness.

Healthy fats

Grapes are a lovely sweet treat that also gives your body what it needs.

AVOCADO
Sometimes called "alligator pears", avocados are filled with healthy fats.

BROCCOLI
Not only is broccoli one of the healthiest foods you can eat, it's much tastier than people give it credit for! It's packed with amazing ANTIOXIDANTS that can help protect the cells in your body from all sorts of nasty baddies.

Vitamin K

GREEN BEANS

Great green beans are a source of healthy natural chemicals found in plants (phytochemicals). If you cook green beans for too long they will lose a lot of their benefits. Plus, nobody likes a soggy bean!

Green beans are great in stirfrys!

ASPARAGUS
Vitamin K is good for the bloodstream. These spears are full of it.

Vitamin C

I'm also a great source of POTASSIUM.

PEAS are great, whether they're fresh or frozen.

SPINACH AND FILO TARTS

Superhero spinach to the rescue! These simple tarts are easy to make for an afternoon snack or as part of a main meal. Try crumbling feta cheese on each tart to add flavour and extra dairy into your diet.

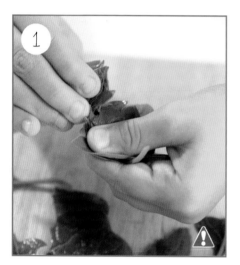

PREHEAT THE OVEN to 180°C (350°F/Gas 4). Brush a muffin tin with oil and set aside. Tear the spinach and the basil into pieces.

IN A LARGE MIXING BOWL, beat the cream cheese, egg, and grated cheese until smooth. Season with salt and pepper, then stir in the spinach.

CAREFULLY CUT the filo pastry into 16 squares measuring 12.5cm (5in). Brush the squares with a little olive oil.

I help fight disease. I also make you grow big and strong. Spinach rules!

INGREDIENTS

- 1 tbsp olive oil
- 250g (9oz) baby spinach leaves, washed

- 2 tbsp fresh basil
- 250g (9oz) cream cheese
- 1 medium egg, beaten
- 25g (scant 1oz) Cheddar or vegetarian Parmesan cheese, grated
- Salt and freshly ground black pepper
- 250g (9oz) filo pastry

- 50g (1¾ oz) feta cheese, crumbled (optional)

PLACE ONE SQUARE on top of another pastry square at an angle to make a star shape. Repeat this process with the rest of the pastry sheets. You should have enough to make 8 tarts.

GENTLY PLACE the pastry sheets in the muffin tin. Push them into the corners to make them fit.

SPOON THE MIXTURE into the casings and smooth it down with the back of the spoon. Bake them for 25 minutes until the filling has set and the pastry is golden brown.

BLACK BEAN AND GUACAMOLE
QUESADILLA

The humble quesadilla (kay-sa-dee-ya) originated in Mexico. It is either a flour or corn tortilla that is filled with yummy ingredients and pan fried. Here we have used black beans and guacamole, but you can make up your own fillings.

Not only does lime juice stop avocados from turning brown, it's full of Vitamin C. Sailors used to eat limes to prevent a disease called "scurvy".

Avocados are full of good things such as Vitamin E, which helps to keep the cells in your body happy and healthy.

EAT ME before someone else does!

5 mins | **5 mins** | **Serves 2**

INGREDIENTS

- 1 tbsp olive oil
- 1 onion, chopped
- 1 clove garlic, crushed

- 400g (14oz) can black beans, drained
- Salt and freshly ground black pepper
- 1 avocado
- 1 tsp lime juice
- 1 red onion, finely chopped
- 1 tomato, de-seeded and finely chopped
- 1 tbsp coriander, finely chopped

- 2 flour (or corn) tortillas
- 25g (scant 1oz) grated Cheddar cheese

HEAT THE OIL in a pan and add the onion and garlic. Cook gently for a few minutes then add the beans. Season and cook for a further 3 minutes.

CAREFULLY CUT the avocado in half. Remove the stone and scoop out the flesh. Place it in a mixing bowl with the lime juice.

MIX IN THE RED ONION, tomatoes, and coriander and season well with salt and pepper. Mash everything together using a potato masher or fork.

SPREAD THE beans and guacamole on a tortilla and scatter the cheese on top. Place in a warm frying pan over a medium heat and place the second tortilla on top.

PRESS DOWN with a spatula and cook for 2–3 minutes until the tortilla is crispy and the cheese is melting.

ASK AN ADULT to invert the tortilla onto a plate and slide it back into the pan so that the other side can cook for a further 2 minutes.

LEAFY GREEN SALAD

Build up your own veggie army with this fresh green salad. Asparagus, broccoli, and green beans are packed with antioxidants, the wonderful warriors that fight "free radicals" that can harm our body's cells.

SNAP OFF THE BOTTOM part of the asparagus stalks and discard them. Cut the rest of the spears into segments.

The Vitamin K in asparagus spears is good for your bones.

10 mins   5 mins   Serves 4

INGREDIENTS

- 100g (3½oz) asparagus
- 100g (3½oz) green beans, trimmed and halved
- 100g (3½oz) fresh peas
- 100g (3½oz) broccoli, chopped
- 150g (5½oz) green leaves (baby spinach, rocket, watercress)
- 10cm (4in) piece of cucumber, halved lengthways and sliced

DRESSING

- 2 tsp white wine vinegar
- 3 tbsp extra virgin olive oil
- 1 tbsp lemon juice
- 1 tsp honey
- 1 tsp pesto

COOK THE BEANS in boiling water for 2 minutes. Add the asparagus, peas, and broccoli and simmer for 3 minutes. Drain, and rinse in cold water, then drain again.

PLACE ALL THE DRESSING ingredients in a bowl. Whisk with a fork until they have all blended together.

PLACE THE SALAD LEAVES and cucumber in a large bowl. Add the cooked vegetables and drizzle on the dressing. Toss it all together and serve.

Oops, I dropped it!

Broccoli is brilliant for you. It contains nutrients that help keep your heart healthy, and is also full of vitamins.

COURGETTE FRITTATA

This frittata is tasty eaten hot or cold. The eggs are full of protein, which helps build and repair your body, and the fibre in the veggies keeps your digestive system working properly.

POWERFUL protein tower

Courgettes contain POTASSIUM, which is good for controlling blood pressure.

Potatoes are a great source of energy.

25 mins | **40 mins** | **Serves 8**

INGREDIENTS

- 400g (14oz) new potatoes
- 50g (1¾oz) butter
- 1 large onion, finely chopped

- 3 courgettes, thinly sliced
- 1 green pepper, de-seeded and chopped
- 100g (3½oz) spinach
- 8 eggs
- 75g (2½oz) vegetarian Parmesan cheese
- 1 tbsp fresh mint leaves, chopped
- Freshly ground black pepper

All bell peppers start out green and change colour and flavour as they ripen....

COOK THE POTATOES in a saucepan of boiling water for 15 minutes, or until tender. Drain and allow to cool, then cut into chunks.

MELT THE BUTTER in a non-stick pan and cook the onion on a low heat until soft. Add the courgettes and pepper and cook for 3 minutes, stirring occasionally.

PREHEAT THE GRILL. While it's heating up, add the spinach and potatoes and cook for 5 minutes, until the spinach is wilted.

CRACK THE EGGS into a bowl and add the vegetarian Parmesan, mint, and a pinch of pepper. Use a fork to mix everything together.

POUR THE EGG MIXTURE into the pan and set the heat to low. Cook for 5 minutes until the eggs are almost set.

PLACE THE PAN under the preheated grill and cook until brown on top – about 5 minutes. Remove and allow to cool before cutting into slices.

GREEN BEAN STIRFRY

Stirfrying is a way of cooking that helps vegetables keep their nutrients and stay crunchy. This dish is packed with plenty of healthy veg, and the coconut makes it extra yummy.

Green beans are found all across the world. They help boost your immune system, and are a source of fibre and iron.

Broccoli is sometimes called a superfood because it's so full of goodness.

BEANSPROUTS are very filling.

24

INGREDIENTS

⊘ 45 mins ⏱ 10 mins 🍴 Serves 4

- 50g (1¾oz) desiccated coconut, unsweetened
- 2 tbsp sunflower oil
- 6 spring onions, chopped
- 1 garlic clove, sliced
- 1 fennel bulb, sliced, core removed

- 150g (5½oz) small broccoli florets
- 100g (3½oz) green beans, trimmed
- 1 tbsp rice vinegar
- 2 tbsp soy sauce
- 100g (3½oz) beansprouts
- 1 tbsp fresh chopped coriander
- 200g (7oz) wholewheat noodles
- 1 tbsp sesame seeds
- 75g (2½oz) unsalted cashew nuts, toasted

Broccoli and green beans are great together.

1 PLACE THE COCONUT in a jug of warm water. Cover and leave for 20 minutes, then strain the coconut through a sieve and reserve the liquid.

2 HEAT THE OIL in a wok or frying pan and cook the spring onions, garlic, fennel, and broccoli for about 2 minutes, stirring occasionally.

3 ADD THE BEANS and cook for 4–5 minutes. Add the vinegar, soy sauce and 4 tbsps of reserved coconut water. Mix, then cook for 1 minute and take off the heat.

4 ADD THE BEANSPROUTS and the drained coconut. Sprinkle the coriander on top and mix everything together well.

5 COOK AND DRAIN the noodles as instructed on the packet. Spoon a portion into each of your serving bowls.

6 SPOON YOUR STIR FRY on top of the noodles. Sprinkle sesame seeds and cashews on top. This will give the dish a crunchy and interesting texture.

GREEN SMOOTHIE

Grapes are just glorious. They are loaded with goodness and help your blood move around your body. Bananas are equally brilliant – they contain potassium that keeps your heart beating strong. Mix them with spinach and you've got the best combo for a tasty, healthy smoothie.

5 mins · 0 mins · Makes 2-4

INGREDIENTS

- 1 small or ½ large banana
- 75g (2½oz) green grapes
- 60g (2oz) baby spinach
- 150ml (5fl oz) milk
(Use almond milk if preferred)
- 1 tbsp honey
- 1 tbsp almond or peanut butter
- Handful of ice cubes

PEEL THE BANANA and break it into chunks. Put into a blender along with the grapes.

ADD THE SPINACH, milk, honey, nut butter, and a handful of ice cubes to the blender.

BLEND THE MIXTURE until smooth. If it's too thick or not chilled enough just add a few cubes of ice and blend again.

You can adapt the recipe to get a different flavour. Try adding a large pinch of ground cinnamon or even a few fresh mint leaves.

My friend spinach is rich in vitamins, which help to keep your blood healthy.

MEET THE
REDS

WE'RE THE RADICAL REDS and we're known for being bright, cheery, and bursting with flavour. From small to large we include tart raspberries, sweet strawberries, juicy tomatoes, sweet red onions, and rosy red peppers. The darker and richer the red, the more nutrients we contain.

INTENSE and flavoursome.

Reach for THE REDS.

Red onions help to keep your heart healthy as well as reducing high blood pressure.

REACH FOR THE REDS

Red may be the colour of fire and anger, but it's hard to be angry when you're chomping on these vibrant, tasty fruits and vegetables! In fact, the more you eat, the happier (and healthier!) you'll be.

Always eat the skin of a red apple – it's where most of the goodness is!

CHERRIES contain melatonin, which can help you to have a good night's sleep.

RASPBERRIES
Soft, squidgy, and delicious, raspberries are one of the sweetest fruits around.

RED PEPPER

Red peppers are even better than their green and yellow brothers and sisters. This is because the red ones contain more nutrients. Eat them raw, or cook them in a tasty dish – no matter what, they'll lend a helping hand to protect your heart and eyes.

Go ahead, get your REDS!

TOMATOES

All types of tomato contain lovely lycopene. Lycopene is what gives tomatoes their red colour, but more importantly it protects the cells in your body and boosts your immune system. You get more lycopene from cooked tomatoes than raw ones.

Lots of
LYCOPENE

WATERMELONS contain lots of water and fibre that help your digestion.

CHILLIES can be so spicy they'll make you sweat. But that's okay! Herbs and spices add lots of flavour.

RED ONION

Both red and white onions contain lots of a mineral called SULPHUR. It's a great mineral that really helps your blood and can also make your hair healthy and glossy.

Super
SULPHUR

GRAPEFRUITS can taste quite bitter, but they're full of Vitamin C.

I'm a fantastic STRAWBERRY. I start to lose my nutrients as soon as I'm picked, so eat me ASAP!

RED PEPPER HOUMOUS

Red peppers are naturally sweet, and are seriously delicious as an ingredient in a houmous dip. They help add to the texture and the taste. Red peppers are also loaded with Vitamin C.

Yum! These crunchy celery sticks are perfect for dipping into the houmous. It's a wonderful snack.

CHICKPEAS are one of the best sources of protein out there.

20 mins 5 mins Serves 2

INGREDIENTS

- 2 red peppers, plus extras for serving
- 150g (5½oz) canned chickpeas, drained
- 1 tsp paprika
- 1 clove garlic, peeled
- Juice of 1 lemon
- 1 tbsp tahini
- 3 tbsp olive oil
- Salt and freshly ground black pepper
- 1 large carrot, peeled, for serving
- 2 celery stalks for serving
- ½ cucumber for serving
- 2 slices of wholemeal pitta bread, sliced

Garlic is a strong-flavoured vegetable. It helps to keep your heart healthy.

PREHEAT A GRILL to high. Carefully cut the peppers into quarters and take out all of the stalks and seeds.

LINE A BAKING TRAY with foil. Place the peppers on it with the skin side facing up and grill the peppers for 5 minutes, until the skins have blackened.

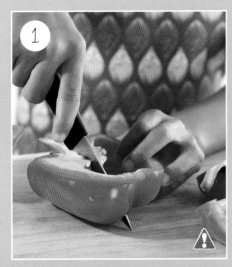

PUT THE PEPPERS in a bag and seal it up. Wait for 10 minutes so the peppers are cool and then peel off the skins. They should come off easily.

PUT THE PEPPERS, chickpeas, paprika, garlic, lemon juice, tahini, and olive oil into a food processor and blend until smooth. Season to taste.

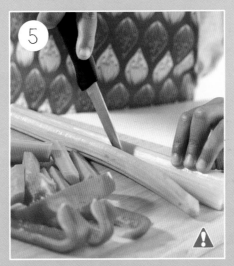

CAREFULLY CUT THE CARROTS, celery, red peppers, and cucumber into sticks.

SPOON THE HOUMOUS into a bowl and serve with the vegetable sticks and toasted pitta bread.

TOMATO SOUP

This is a classic comfort dish for when it's cold outside. Tomatoes are packed with Vitamin C, Vitamin A, and potassium. Did you know that tomatoes are actually a fruit, not a vegetable?

Eat me, and I will help to keep your heart healthy.

20 mins | **35 mins** | **Serves 2-4**

INGREDIENTS

- 4 tbsp olive oil
- 1 small onion, chopped
- 1 small carrot, chopped
- 2 sticks celery, chopped
- 1 garlic clove, crushed
- 1 tbsp plain flour
- 400g (14oz) can chopped tomatoes
- 1 tbsp tomato purée
- 1 tbsp fresh thyme leaves, chopped
- 450ml (15fl oz) vegetable stock
- A pinch of sugar
- Salt and freshly ground pepper

I'm packed with VITAMIN C.

Tomatoes also contain something called "lycopene", which is a powerful antioxidant that helps prevent disease. Lycopene gives tomatoes their deep red colour.

1

HEAT THE OLIVE OIL in a small pan over medium heat then add the onion, carrot, and celery.

2

COOK THE ONION, carrot, and celery for about 5 minutes until they soften, then stir in the garlic and the flour and cook for another minute.

3

ADD THE TINNED TOMATOES, tomato purée, thyme, stock, and sugar. Bring the mixture to the boil then reduce to a low heat and simmer for 25 minutes.

4

REMOVE THE SOUP from the heat and allow to cool a little. Ladle it into a blender and blend until smooth. Pour back into a pan to reheat before serving. Season with salt and freshly ground pepper.

TOMATO
AND ONION TARTS

These tarts are surprisingly filling. When cooked, puff pastry rises and leaves air pockets inside, making it light and fluffy. Puff pastry can be used for savoury or sweet dishes.

Help me sprinkle more of these basil leaves on top. They add to the flavour!

Totally tasty
TARTS

INGREDIENTS

- 375g (13oz) ready-prepared puff pastry
- 250g (9oz) cherry tomatoes
- 250g (9oz) ricotta cheese
- 2 eggs, beaten
- 2 tbsp freshly chopped basil
- 25g (scant 1oz) vegetarian Parmesan (or mozzarella) cheese, grated
- Salt and freshly ground black pepper
- 1 red onion, sliced

Cherry tomatoes are high in Vitamin A and Vitamin B6.

PREHEAT THE OVEN to 200°C (400°F/Gas 6). On a lightly floured surface roll the pastry out into a rectangle measuring 25x38cm (10x15in).

USE A KNIFE to cut six equal squares of pastry then score a 1cm (½in) border around the edges. Transfer the squares onto a greased baking tray.

SLICE THE CHERRY TOMATOES in half. A serrated knife can make this easier if you have one.

Scatter fresh basil leaves on top of each tart.

IN A LARGE MIXING BOWL, mix the ricotta, eggs, basil, and Parmesan (or mozzarella). Season with salt and pepper.

SPREAD THE MIXTURE on the squares, making sure to stay inside the borders. Scatter the tomatoes and onion on top and bake for 20 minutes or until golden.

VEGGIE LASAGNE

A hearty, lovely lasagne is packed tight with good, colourful veggies. The pretty, purple aubergine adds to the texture, contains Vitamins B1 and B6, and is filled with fibre.

They may make you cry, but onions really help your health. Red ones are the sweetest.

Peppers contain loads of Vitamins A and C. Did you know that Vitamin A can help your eyesight?

50 mins   1hr 15 mins   Serves 6

INGREDIENTS

- 2 large red onions, peeled
- 2 courgettes
- 2 large carrots, peeled
- 4 red peppers, de-seeded
- 175g (6oz) mushrooms, halved or quartered depending on the size
- 1 medium aubergine
- 2 garlic cloves, crushed
- 2 tbsp rosemary, chopped
- 4 tbsp olive oil
- 400g (14oz) can of chopped tomatoes
- 1 tbsp tomato purée
- 1 tsp dried oregano
- Salt and freshly ground black pepper
- 60g (2oz) unsalted butter
- 30g (1oz) plain flour
- 500ml (16fl oz) warm milk
- 100g (3½oz) vegetarian Parmesan cheese, grated
- 10 dried lasagne sheets

PREHEAT THE OVEN to 220°C (425°F/Gas 7). Cut the onions, courgettes, carrots, peppers, mushrooms, and aubergine into chunks.

PLACE THE CUT veggies in an ovenproof dish. Add the garlic, rosemary, and oil. Toss together, then roast for 30 minutes. Turn the veg over halfway through.

COOK THE TOMATOES, tomato purée, and oregano over a low heat for 15 minutes. Season and stir in the vegetables, then take off the heat.

MELT THE BUTTER over a low heat and stir in the flour. Cook for 1 minute then slowly whisk in the milk a little at a time until it has thickened. Add half the cheese.

REDUCE THE OVEN'S temperature to 190°C (375°F/Gas 5). Spoon a third of the vegetable mixture into a lasagne dish and top with 3 lasagne sheets.

ADD ANOTHER THIRD of the vegetable mix and lasagne sheets. Top with half of the sauce, then the remaining vegetables.

LAY ON THE FINAL lasagne sheets, then spread the remaining sauce on top. Sprinkle on the remaining cheese and bake for 35 minutes, until golden.

VERY BERRY PLUM PIE

Berries and plums have their own natural sugars that bring a delicious sweet flavour to this puffy pie. Serve with a scoop of ice-cream to take this treat to the next level.

1hr 15 mins | 30 mins | Serves 6-8

INGREDIENTS

- 500g (1lb 2oz) ready-prepared puff pastry
- Flour for dusting
- 1 egg, beaten

- 650g (1lb 6oz) mixed berries – raspberries and strawberries
- 2 tbsp caster sugar
- 2 tbsp cornflour
- 200g (7oz) plums, stoned and cut into quarters
- Icing sugar for dusting

1 PREHEAT THE OVEN to 200°C (400°F/Gas 6). On a lightly floured surface, roll out the puff pastry until it's about 5mm (¼in) thick.

2 LAY A 25cm (10in) PLATE on the pastry and cut around it. Move the circle onto a baking sheet and brush all over the surface with a little beaten egg.

Strawberries are great. One handful contains as much Vitamin C as a whole orange!

3 COMBINE THE BERRIES, sugar, cornflour, and plums in a mixing bowl. Gently toss to coat, being careful not to crush the fruit.

Here we go!

Come on, DIVE IN!

SPOON THE FRUIT in the middle of the pastry, leaving a 7.5cm (3in) border around the outside. Scrunch up the edges and bring them towards the centre, leaving the middle uncovered.

PLACE IN THE FRIDGE for 30 minutes to chill. Brush the crust with the leftover beaten egg, then place the pie into the oven.

BAKE THE PIE for 30 minutes until golden brown, rotating halfway through cooking. Allow 30 minutes to cool, then dust with icing sugar and serve.

MEET THE PURPLES

PERFECT AND PROUD, the purples are happy
to tell you just how wonderful they are and
how they can help prevent you getting poorly.
This group includes awesome aubergines,
brilliant blackberries, bold beetroot, great grapes,
breathtaking blueberries, and remarkable raisins.

Aren't we
PRETTY?!

Pick the
PURPLES

I help to increase
immunity, improve
heart health, and lower
the risk of disease.

PICK UP THE PURPLES

Fruit and veg that are purple and dark blue are linked to keeping the HEART healthy and the BRAIN functioning at its best. They also help protect the body from disease, improve MEMORY, and increase blood circulation.

BLACKBERRIES
These berries are high in FIBRE which aids digestion. They are also full of Vitamin K which promotes good bone health.

FIGS
This sweet little fruit is a great source of FIBRE, vitamins, and MINERALS.

PURPLE GRAPES
contain powerful ANTIOXIDANTS.

AUBERGINE

Not only is this mighty warrior full of fibre, it also boasts high levels of Vitamin C. It is healthy as it's low in fat and can help to remove excess iron in the body. It might sound surprising, but aubergines are actually a very large berry — so they're fruit, not veg.

I'm great at soaking up lots of other great flavours.

BLUEBERRIES

These delicious berries are high in FIBRE as well as Vitamin E and C. They're full of wonderful antioxidants that protect you from disease, and research has shown that they boost brain activity.

PLUMS are full of Vitamin B.

Fibre

PURPLE CABBAGE
This veg is commonly called "red cabbage". It's really high in Vitamin A.

RAISINS
Did you know that raisins are dried grapes? They're tasty to eat raw.

BEETROOT

Although it can be eaten raw, beetroot is usually cooked or pickled before being eaten. The leaves are rich in calcium, iron, and vitamins and the roots are a source of FOLIC ACID, which can help your body to build new cells.

Vitamin C

FRUITY RAISIN GRANOLA

Breakfast is the most important meal of the day, and a great way to get a healthy energy boost. Raisins and berries are high in fibre, and they're a great way to kick start your morning.

Nom nom nom!

Blackberries have their own natural sweeteners, and provide you with lots of Vitamin C.

5 mins | 30 mins | Serves 8–10

INGREDIENTS

- 115g (4oz) mixed nuts (hazelnuts, walnuts, almonds)
- 350g (12oz) rolled oats
- 60g (2oz) pumpkin seeds
- 60g (2oz) sunflower seeds
- 2 tbsp sunflower oil
- 8 tbsp honey
- 115g (4oz) raisins
- Blackberries to serve
- Milk or yogurt to serve

1

PREHEAT THE OVEN to 160°C (325°F/Gas 3). Put the nuts in a plastic bag and crush them with a rolling pin. In a large mixing bowl, combine the nuts, oats, and seeds.

2

IN A SMALL JUG mix together the oil and honey, then pour it into the bowl of oats and seeds. Use a spoon to stir the mixture until it's all combined.

3

SPOON THE MIXTURE on to 2 baking trays in a single layer, then bake in the oven for 15 minutes. Turn the mixture over and bake for an extra 15 minutes.

4

ALLOW THE MIXTURE TO COOL, then tip into a bowl. Mix in the raisins and transfer into an airtight container to store. Serve in a bowl with yoghurt and blackberries.

RAINBOW SALAD

All the colours in this book are shown off in this signature salad. Have fun building the layers that make up a beautiful and edible rainbow. Packed with vitamins, protein, and plenty of fibre, it's sure to become a family favourite.

25 mins | 5 mins | Serves 4

INGREDIENTS

- 2 tsp sesame oil
- 2 tsp rice vinegar
- 1 tbsp soy sauce
- 2 tsp honey
- 2 tbsp extra virgin olive oil
- 400g (14oz) tofu (one block)
- 225g (8oz) freshly podded peas, or frozen peas thawed
- Small handful mint leaves, torn
- 12 cherry tomatoes, halved
- 2 carrots, 200g (7oz) peeled and grated
- A yellow and an orange pepper, cut into strips
- 2 beetroot, 200g (7oz) peeled and grated
- Mixed salad leaves
- 1 tbsp toasted sesame seeds

You can make these salads ahead of time and take them on a picnic. They're perfect!

Beat the winter blues with beetroot. It's full of Vitamin C, so can help you to get over a cold more quickly.

Layers of GOODNESS

1. TO MAKE THE DRESSING, place the sesame oil, rice vinegar, soy sauce, honey, and 1 tbsp extra virgin olive oil in a sealable jar and shake until well mixed.

2. PLACE THE TOFU on a plate lined with kitchen paper. Place more paper and a chopping board on top. Leave for 15 minutes to help squeeze out any liquid.

3. CUT THE TOFU into 2.5cm (1in) cubes. Heat the remaining olive oil in a frying pan ready to cook the tofu.

4. ASK AN ADULT to cook the tofu on a medium heat until it has browned on all sides, this will take about 5 minutes.

5. MAKE UP THE LAYERS of salad in a glass or jar. Begin with the peas and mint, then add a layer of tomatoes, carrot, yellow and orange peppers.

6. ADD A LAYER OF beetroot, tofu, and salad leaves. When you're ready to eat, add a little of the dressing, shake to combine, then top with the sesame seeds.

AUBERGINE
AND TOMATO BAKE

Dig into the layers of delicious goodness. The main ingredients that make this recipe are amazing aubergines and terrific tomatoes. Did you know that aubergines and tomatoes are both fruits?

Join us in our healthy feast. Aubergines are high in fibre, and contain potassium.

Super-tasty TOPPING

30 mins | **1 hr** | **Serves 4**

INGREDIENTS

- 4 tbsp extra virgin olive oil
- 1 medium onion, finely chopped
- 2 garlic cloves, finely chopped
- 2 x 400g (14oz) cans chopped tomatoes
- 1 tsp dried oregano
- 1 tsp sugar
- 2 medium aubergines, approx. 600g (1lb 5oz)
- Salt and freshly ground black pepper
- 100g (3½oz) grated mozzarella cheese

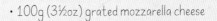

Aubergines are called "eggplants" in the USA.

PREHEAT THE OVEN to 190°C (375°F/Gas 5). Heat 1 tbsp of oil in a pan and cook the onion for 5 minutes. Add the garlic and cook a further minute.

ADD THE TOMATOES to the pan. Add the oregano and sugar and season with salt and pepper. Bring to a simmer and cook for 20 minutes.

CUT THE AUBERGINE into slices 5mm (¼in) thick. Brush the aubergine slices on each side with the remaining oil and season with salt and pepper.

HEAT A GRIDDLE PAN, then working in batches over a medium heat, brown the aubergines for 2–3 minutes on each side until tender. Set aside.

DIVIDE A THIRD of the tomato sauce into 4 dishes, then add 3–4 slices of aubergine. Repeat this process then finish with a layer of sauce on the top.

SCATTER THE CHEESE over the top. Cook in the oven to bake for 25 minutes or until the tops are golden brown and bubbling.

LAYERED BERRY CHEESECAKES

Juicy blueberries and blackberries go really well with the crumbly, crushed biscuits in this dish. These cheesecakes are best when very cold, so only take them out of the fridge just before you're ready to serve them.

1 hr 20 mins | 5 mins | Serves 4

INGREDIENTS

- 300g (10oz) blueberries
- 250g (9oz) blackberries
- 2 tbsp caster sugar
- 250g (9oz) cream cheese
- 200ml (7fl oz) crème fraîche
- 1 tsp non-alcoholic vanilla extract
- 100g (3½ oz) oat biscuits, crushed

Chilled and RELAXED

Blueberries and blackberries both contain natural chemicals that can help to protect you from disease.

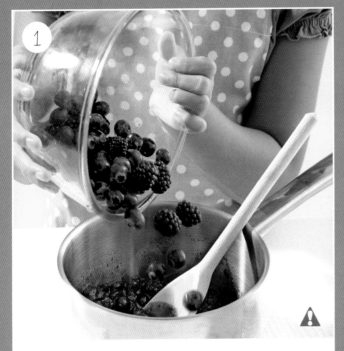

PLACE TWO THIRDS of the berries and 1 tbsp of sugar in a medium pan. Add a lid and cook over a low heat for 5 minutes. Stir in the remaining berries and leave to cool.

BEAT THE REMAINING 1 tbsp sugar, cream cheese, crème fraîche, and vanilla extract in a bowl. Do this until the mixture is soft and creamy.

START TO LAYER UP the cheesecakes. In glasses or a jar, create a layer of berry sauce, then the cream cheese mixture, then the biscuits. Repeat until you're finished.

DOT THE REMAINING fresh berries on top then place the cheesecakes into the fridge for an hour to allow them to set. Share them with your friends!

MEET THE YELLOWS

Hi there! We're good at all sorts of things, but we're best known for our ability to aid brain function and help with digestion. The yellow clan are made up of tasty bananas, powerful pineapples, juicy yellow peppers, scrumptious sweetcorn, zingy lemons, and of course... the humble potato.

Yummy YELLOWS

Bright and BOLD

I increase your immunity, give you healthy skin, and help to prevent heart disease.

SAY YES TO YELLOWS

It's easy to feel mellow if you eat lots of yellow. The outsides may look sunny and powerful, but it's the insides that have the real power – the power to boost your immune system that is!

PEACHES are naturally sweet and succulent. They're perfect with cereal or in a smoothie.

You can do so much with POTATOES, but it's often healthiest to bake or steam them. They fill you up and are a good source of energy.

PEPPERS start off green, then change colour as they ripen. All the colours taste slightly different.

SUPER spud

LEMONS

Not only do lemons bring vibrant flavour to a dish, they bring loads of Vitamin C to your body. Sailors used to eat lemons to avoid a disease called scurvy.

HONEYDEW MELON is yummy at breakfast or as dessert

BANANAS

According to scientists, bananas make you happy! This is because they contain amino acids that boost your serotonin – a chemical that makes you feel happy. Bananas also contain a special kind of fibre which encourages friendly bacteria in the gut.

CORN

Crunchy yellow corn is a brain food. It contains Vitamin B1, which is also known as thiamine. Thiamine is a fantastic memory booster, and can improve your everyday thinking – so eat corn before you do your homework!

Tasty and TROPICAL

PINEAPPLES
Spiky on the outside, but sweet on the inside, pineapples take over a year to grow. Good things come to those who wait!

For thousands of years people have used GARLIC as a way to prevent illnesses. Cook with it the next time you have a cold!

PEPPER
AND QUINOA SALAD

15 mins 20 mins Serves 4

INGREDIENTS

- 3 yellow peppers, de-seeded and chopped
- 1 medium red onion, thickly sliced
- 2 courgettes, halved lengthways and sliced
- 225g (8oz) small cauliflower florets
- 12 cherry tomatoes
- 2 tbsp olive oil
- Salt and freshly ground black pepper
- 125g (4½oz) quinoa
- 300ml (10fl oz) vegetable stock
- Handful of basil leaves, chopped
- Handful of parsley leaves, chopped

This healthy salad contains such a variety of colourful ingredients. Quinoa is a healthy seed that's high in protein, and contains fibre. If you can't find quinoa, couscous will work just as well.

PUSH, PUSH. Get it to the dinner table!

1 PREHEAT THE OVEN to 200°C (400°F/ Gas 6). Place the peppers, onions, courgettes, cauliflower, and tomatoes in a roasting tin. Coat with oil and season with salt and pepper.

2 ROAST THE VEG in the oven for 20 minutes. While they're roasting, place the quinoa in a sieve and rinse it under the tap. If you don't the quinoa can taste bitter.

3 TIP THE QUINOA into a saucepan and add a pinch of salt. Stir over a medium heat for 1 minute so the water evaporates and the quinoa toasts slightly.

The herbs adds FLAVOUR

POUR THE VEGETABLE STOCK into the pan and bring to a boil. Reduce it to a simmer then cover and allow the quinoa to cook for 15 minutes.

REMOVE FROM THE HEAT and leave it covered for another 5 minutes to rest. This is an important step as it will make the quinoa fluffy instead of soggy.

TRANSFER THE QUINOA into a large bowl and fluff it up with a fork. Add the roasted vegetables along with the fresh basil and parsley. Serve warm or cold.

BEAN AND CORN BAKE

This is an incredibly satisfying meal that's similar to the Greek dish "moussaka". The creamy egg and yoghurt mixture creates a delicious and fluffy topping. Serve with a salad to add extra colours from the food rainbow.

Cannellini beans are full of fibre and protein. Every cell in your body needs protein.

Yellow food, such as corn, helps your skin and eyes stay healthy.

15 mins **35 mins** **Serves 4-6**

INGREDIENTS

- 1 tbsp olive oil
- 1 onion, finely chopped
- 2 x 400g (14oz) cans chopped tomatoes
- 1 tbsp tomato purée
- 3 tsp dried oregano
- 400g (14oz) can cannellini beans, drained and rinsed
- 1 x 200g (7oz) can corn, drained and rinsed
- 3 tbsp freshly chopped parsley
- 250ml (9fl oz) Greek-style yoghurt
- 1 egg
- Small handful of vegetarian Parmesan cheese
- Salad, to serve

1 PREHEAT THE OVEN to 200°C (400°F/Gas 6). Heat the oil in a pan and cook the onion over a medium heat for 4–5 minutes or until it becomes soft.

2 ADD THE CHOPPED TOMATOES, tomato purée, and 1 tsp of oregano. Bring to the boil then reduce and simmer for about 10 minutes. Stir in the beans and corn and cook for 5 minutes. Then add the parsley.

3 PUT THE YOGHURT, egg, and remaining 2 tbsp oregano into a bowl and stir until well mixed.

4 SPOON THE BEAN MIXTURE into an ovenproof dish then spoon the yoghurt mixture on top. Sprinkle the Parmesan on top then bake in the oven for 20 minutes, or until the top is golden and set.

CORNBREAD MOUNTAIN

Boiling vegetables can destroy some of the vitamins, so it's best to eat them raw, steamed, or baked, like the corn in this recipe. The cornmeal is like a grainy yellow flour. It's made from ground corn kernels.

Reach for THE SKY!

Corn and cornmeal are high in fibre.

Corn is a good source of B vitamins, which help to keep the blood healthy.

10 mins   20–25 mins   Serves 9–16

INGREDIENTS

- 20g (¾oz) butter for greasing
- 125g (4½oz) plain flour
- 125g (4½oz) cornmeal/polenta
- 1 tbsp baking powder
- 1 tsp salt
- 5 spring onions, thinly chopped
- 175g (6oz) drained corn
- 2 eggs
- 50g (1¾oz) butter, melted and cooled
- 350ml (12fl oz) milk

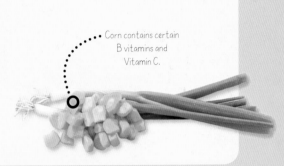

Corn contains certain B vitamins and Vitamin C.

1 PREHEAT THE OVEN to 200°C (400°F/Gas 6). Grease a 23cm (9in) square baking tin with butter.

2 MIX THE FLOUR, cornmeal/polenta, baking powder, salt, spring onions, and sweetcorn in a large bowl.

3 IN ANOTHER BOWL, whisk the eggs, cooled melted butter, and milk until thoroughly combined.

4 POUR THE WET INGREDIENTS into the dry ones and stir with a wooden spoon until everything is nicely mixed.

5 POUR THE MIXTURE into the baking tin and bake in the oven for 25–30 minutes until golden brown.

6 ALLOW TO COOL before cutting into slices or squares. Cornbread makes for a lovely savoury snack.

63

SUNSHINE RICE

Rice is a hugely popular ingredient all over the world. In some countries it's eaten at every meal! Rice gives you lots of energy as it's high in carbohydrates. It goes so well with veggies!

There are lots of different types of rice. Brown rice is the best source of fibre.

Light and BRIGHT

5 mins | 30 mins | Serves 4

INGREDIENTS

- 1 tbsp olive oil
- 1 onion, chopped
- 200g (7oz) long grain rice
- 1 tsp turmeric
- 1 green or red chilli, de-seeded and finely chopped
- 1 large clove garlic, finely chopped
- 750ml (1¼pint) hot vegetable stock
- 400g (14oz) can red kidney beans, rinsed and drained
- 3 large vine tomatoes
- 1 red and 1 green pepper, de-seeded and cubed
- 50g (1¾oz) frozen peas
- 4 spring onions, chopped

HEAT THE OIL in a large pan and cook the onion over a gentle heat for 2-3 minutes until softened.

ADD THE RICE, turmeric, chilli, and garlic to coat in the oil. Cook for 2 minutes, stirring constantly.

Our friend turmeric is a spice that provides this dish with flavour and colour. It's used as a type of medicine in parts of the world.

ADD THE STOCK and kidney beans to the pan and stir to combine. Cover the pan and simmer for 15 minutes, stirring occasionally.

CUT A CROSS at each end of the tomatoes and place in a bowl. Cover with boiling water for a minute then let cool. Peel off the skins, then cut into chunks and take out the seeds.

ADD THE TOMATOES, peppers, peas, and spring onions and cook, covered for 10 more minutes stirring twice, until the rice has absorbed the stock and is creamy.

LEMON
DRIZZLE CAKE

This lovely loaf cake is both sweet and sour at the same time. Lemons are loaded with Vitamin C, and can be a real boost to your immune system. The skin of a lemon, called the zest, is really good too.

25 mins | 45–50 mins | Serves 8

INGREDIENTS

- 20g (¾oz) butter for greasing
- Finely grated zest of 2 unwaxed lemons
- 200g (7oz) butter, softened
- 200g (7oz) caster sugar
- 3 eggs, beaten
- 200g (7oz) self-raising flour, sifted
- 1 tsp baking powder
- 2 tbsp milk
- Juice 2 lemons
- 75g (2½oz) granulated sugar
- 85g (3oz) icing sugar

I make the cake moist and full of a yummy fresh flavour.

1 PREHEAT THE OVEN to 180°C (350°C/Gas 4). Grease a loaf tin and line the base with baking paper so the cake won't stick.

2 PLACE THE ZEST of 2 lemons, butter, and caster sugar in a mixing bowl and beat until the mixture is light and fluffy.

3 WHISK IN THE EGGS, a little at a time. Sift the flour and baking powder together then fold into the mixture with the milk. Put the mixture in the tin.

4 BAKE THE CAKE in the centre of the oven for 45–50 minutes or until a cocktail stick comes out clean. Prick the top of the cake with the cocktail stick.

5 MIX 4 tsp OF THE LEMON JUICE with the granulated sugar in a bowl. Drizzle the sugary juice over the cake so it sinks into all the holes. Allow the cake to cool before turning it out.

6 COMBINE THE ICING SUGAR with the rest of the lemon juice and mix until smooth. Drizzle the icing over the top, allowing it to run over the sides.

MEET THE ORANGES

WE'RE VIVID AND VIBRANT! The oranges rule when it comes to helping you have a healthy heart. Orange fruit and veg increase your immunity. The orange tribe includes tasty sweet potatoes, perfect peaches, perky pumpkins, cool carrots, brilliant butternut squash, and incredibly juicy oranges.

Big and
BOLD

Eat your
ORANGES

I can help to strengthen your bones and improve your digestion.

GO OVERBOARD FOR ORANGES

Bold and brilliant – orange food tends to contain a lot of something called "beta-carotene". In your body this turns into Vitamin A, which is good for your eyes. Orange food can also contain Vitamin C, which helps protect you from illness.

PAPAYA is a fruit that grows in warm places. It's full of vitamins and minerals.

You can buy sweet potatoes that are white or orange on the inside. The orange ones taste sweeter.

Tough on the outside, but smooth and tasty on the inside. BUTTERNUT SQUASH is hearty and nutritious. Even the seeds are good for you!

SWEET POTATO

Both potatoes and sweet potatoes are filling, packed with nutrients, and give you lots of energy, but sweet potatoes have loads more Vitamin A.

CARROTS

So much more than "rabbit food", carrots are amazing. There's an old rumour that carrots make you see in the dark. That's not exactly true, but their beta-carotene (the clue's in the name!) does help to keep your eyes healthy.

TANGERINES are smaller and easier to peel than oranges. Both have plenty of vitamins.

Fresh APRICOTS contain useful antioxidants. Dried apricots taste great, but can contain lots of sugar.

MANGO

Known as the "king of fruit" in some parts of the world, Sweet, tasty mangoes are rich in Vitamin C and beta-carotene. No wonder so many people love them!

Awesome
PUMPKIN

PUMPKIN isn't just for carving at Halloween! Eating it helps to reduce blood pressure.

71

SWEET POTATO OMELETTE

Traditionally made with regular potatoes, this Spanish-style omelette, or tortilla, uses healthier sweet potatoes instead. Sweet potatoes are a versatile veg and they taste great baked, boiled, or fried.

Superhero? More like SUPERFOOD!

Eating me can improve your EYE SIGHT.

15 mins

15 mins

Serves 4

INGREDIENTS

- 2 sweet potatoes 450g (1lb), peeled and sliced 5mm (¼in) thick

- 2 tbsp olive oil

- 30g (1oz) butter

- 5 spring onions, trimmed and chopped

- 1 yellow or orange pepper, de-seeded and sliced

- 2 tbsp fresh thyme leaves, plus extra to garnish

- Salt and freshly ground black pepper

- 6 eggs, beaten

BRING WATER IN A SAUCEPAN to the boil and cook the sweet potato slices for about 5 minutes until tender but still holding their shape. Drain carefully in a colander.

HEAT THE OIL and butter in a large non-stick pan. Add the spring onions and pepper and cook over a medium heat for about 2 minutes.

ADD THE SWEET POTATOES, thyme, salt and pepper, then stir gently to combine. Add the eggs and cover the pan with a lid. Cook over a medium low heat for about 5 minutes, until almost set.

MEANWHILE, PREHEAT THE GRILL. When it's hot, put the frying pan under it for a few minutes until the egg is set and the top is golden brown. Sprinkle thyme on top and slide the omelette onto a plate.

CARROT AND ORANGE TREATS

Juicy oranges and tasty carrots are a perfect duo in this "orange" treat. Carrots contain beta-carotene, which boosts the immune system. Oranges are high in Vitamin C and A. They're good for your heart and skin.

20 mins | **25 mins** | **Makes 12**

INGREDIENTS

- 140g (5oz) plain flour
- 2 tsp baking powder
- ½ tsp bicarbonate of soda
- 85g (3oz) light brown sugar
- 50g (1¾oz) hazelnuts, chopped
- 1 tbsp poppy seeds
- 100g (3½oz) carrot, grated
- 60g (2oz) sultanas
- ½ tsp ground cinnamon
- 100g (3½oz) porridge oats
- Zest and juice of 1 large orange
- 200ml (7fl oz) buttermilk
- 1 egg, beaten
- 75g (2½oz) butter, melted
- Pinch of salt

The top has a golden brown crunchy texture... ready and waiting for you to tuck in. Yum!

74

PREHEAT THE OVEN to 200°C (400°F/Gas 6). In a large bowl, combine the flour, baking powder, bicarbonate of soda, and sugar. Stir in the nuts, poppy seeds carrot, sultanas, cinnamon, oats, and orange zest.

IN A SECOND BOWL, mix the buttermilk, egg, butter, salt, and orange juice. Mix with a spatula then pour the wet ingredients onto the dry.

USE A SPATULA to gently fold the mixture together. Be careful not to mix it too much or it won't end up light and fluffy.

LINE MUFFIN TINS with 12 muffin cases, then spoon the mixture into the cases – filling them up about two-thirds of the way. Bake for 20–25 minutes. Transfer to a wire rack to cool.

BUTTERNUT SQUASH SOUP

There's nothing else like a tasty bowl of soup on a chilly day. The smaller a squash is the more flavour it will have, so don't always choose the biggest one. Butternut squash is similar to pumpkin. Did you know they're both fruits, not vegetables?

Orange peppers are loaded with Vitamin A and C. The content of Vitamin C is higher if eaten when fully ripe.

1, 2, 3...
...LIFT!

Butternut squash contains many different vitamins and minerals, as well as lots of fibre. It releases energy slowly, and keeps your blood sugar levels stable.

15 mins | 40 mins | Serves 4

INGREDIENTS

- 1kg (2¼lb) butternut squash
- 2 medium carrots, approximately 200g (7oz)
- 1 orange pepper, de-seeded and chopped
- 1 tbsp vegetable oil
- 1 onion, roughly chopped
- 1 litre (1¾ pint) vegetable stock
- Toasted pumpkin seeds (optional)

Put your back into it guys!

1 PREHEAT THE OVEN to 200°C (400°F/Gas 6). Cut the butternut squash in half lengthways and scoop out the seeds and pith from the centre.

2 CAREFULLY REMOVE the skin with a peeler. Cut the squash into small cubes about 2cm (¾in) in size. Peel and roughly chop the carrots.

3 PLACE THE PEPPER, carrots, and squash cubes in a roasting tray and drizzle oil on top. Season with salt and pepper, then roast for 20 minutes.

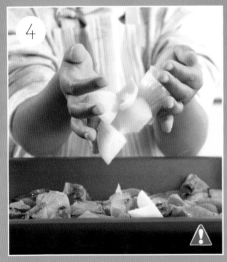

4 REMOVE FROM THE OVEN and add the onion. Return the baking tray to the oven for a further 15 minutes. Remove and allow to cool slightly.

5 PLACE THE VEGETABLES and half the stock in a food processor and blend until smooth. Or you can mash the squash with a potato masher.

6 POUR THE MIXTURE back into a saucepan, add the rest of the stock and simmer for 3-4 minutes until hot. Serve with a sprinkling of pumpkin seeds on top.

MANGO AND COCONUT POPS

Mangoes are naturally sweet, and full of fibre, copper, and Vitamin C. These refreshing little lollies are the perfect treat on a hot summer's day.

Super CHILLED!

Coconut milk is really nutritious. Coconuts are high in fibre, and contain lots of vitamins and minerals.

2-3 hours | 0 mins | Makes 6-8

INGREDIENTS

- 1 ripe mango
- 400ml (14fl oz) can coconut milk
- 2 tbsp honey
- Juice of 2 limes

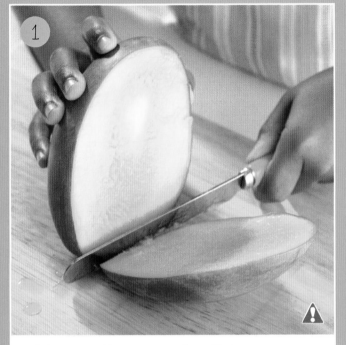

1

ASK AN ADULT to slice the lobes off the mango, guiding the knife around the stone in the middle.

2

SCORE A DIAMOND criss-cross pattern on the lobes, then turn it inside out to create a hedgehog shape from the mango chunks. Cut off the mango chunks.

3

PLACE THE MANGO, coconut milk, honey, and lime juice in a blender and blend until smooth.

4

POUR THE MIX into lolly moulds, but don't fill them all the way to the top. Place a stick in the middle of each one and freeze for 2–3 hours.

INDEX

Eat me again soon!

DK WOULD LIKE TO THANK

Caryn Jenner for proofreading, Eleanor Bates, Rachael Hare, Charlotte Milner, and Artie the dog for help with photoshoots. Sadie Thomas for the illustrations. Lucy Claxton and Laura Evans for picture library assistance. Barney Allen, Lindsay Guzman, Egypt Hanson, Rio Lewis, Grace Merchant, Liberty Moore, and Olivia Phokou for modelling.

ACKNOWLEDGEMENTS

The publisher would like to thank the following for their kind permission to reproduce their photographs:

(Key: a-above; b-below/bottom; c-centre; f-far; l-left; r-right; t-top)

14 Joanne Doran (c) Dorling Kindersley, Courtesy of RHS Hampton Court Flower Show 2011

All other images © Dorling Kindersley

For further information see: www.dkimages.com

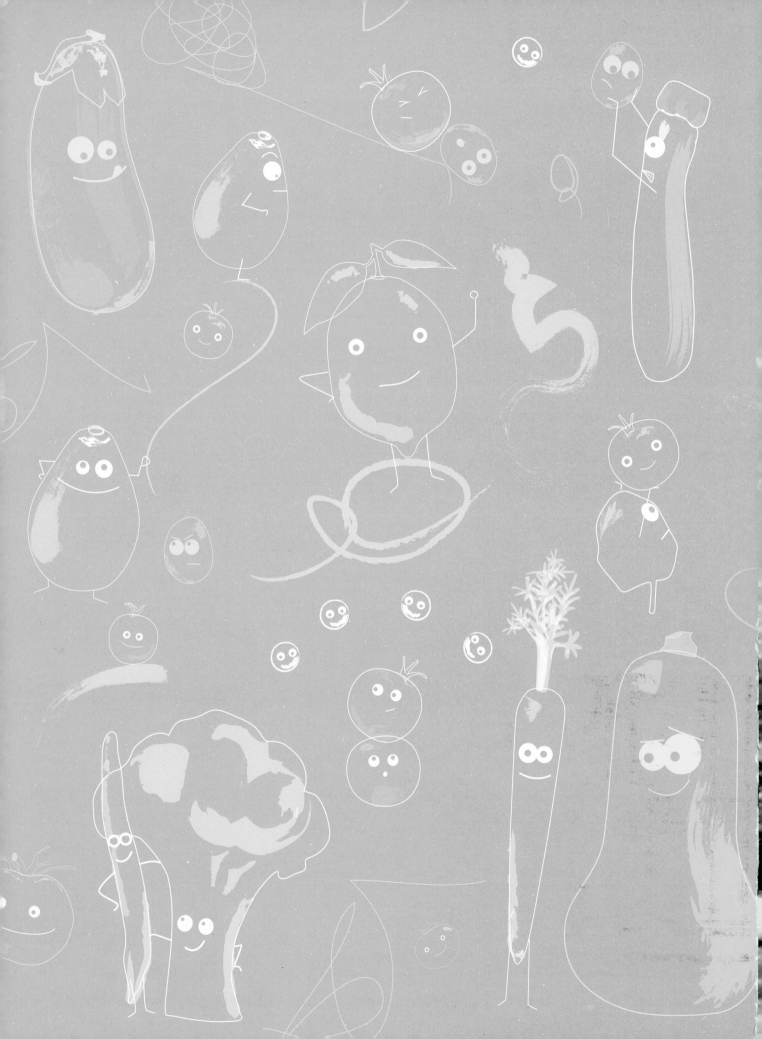